A "Tankful" Armadillo

by Chris Mills

Illustrations by
John Fraser

Copyright © 2017 Chris Mills
Copyright © 2017 TEACH Services, Inc.
ISBN-13: 978-1-4796-0735-8 (Paperback)
ISBN-13: 978-1-4796-0736-5 (iBooks)
ISBN-13: 978-1-4796-0737-2 (Kindle Fire)
Library of Congress Control No: 2017910645

TEACH Services, Inc.
PUBLISHING
www.TEACHServices.com • (800) 367-1844

Fred woke up with a jolt.

"Today is the day I'm digging my new swimming pool! I can already imagine sitting in the cool, crystal blue water to get away from the summer's blazing heat!"

He enthusiastically leaped from his bed and ran for the door.

"Wait!" yelled Frederica, Fred's wife. "Where do you think you're going? You're still in your pajamas, and you haven't eaten your breakfast!"

"Oh, yeah, I forgot!" replied Fred, releasing the door handle and heading back toward the table.

Fred greedily gulped down a quick breakfast of grits and grapes and speedily changed into his dirty but sturdy work clothes.

Then, he headed out toward his Caterpillar D10N bulldozer equipped with a single shank ripper and universal blade. He hopped into the squishy leather captain's chair and turned the key. It started up with a kitty-like purr, well, maybe more like a tiger's roar. Fred jerked a metal lever that made the machine surge forward.

He headed toward a nearby hill and started plowing it flat. As he lifted a bucket full of soil, he noticed five small, roundish, gray objects rolling back and forth in the dirt. With a sudden jerk, they bounced up and out of the bucket and fell all the way to the ground. Four lay still as stones and another grew legs and ran off.

Frantically, Fred jumped off the bulldozer and ran to where the four things lay. What he saw next surprised him. Were they clumps of dirt? Were they bundles of grass? No! The four gray objects were baby armadillos! One of them lay lifeless, and the others were cuddled together in a tight ball scared out of their wits.

Fred realized he had accidentally dug up an armadillo den. Their mother never returned to gct the remaining armadillos, leaving Fred with three hungry baby orphans.

Fred didn't have any experience taking care of armadillos and didn't know what to feed one, so he decided to call an experienced animal rehabilitator, Andrea White. Since Andrea loved animals of all kinds so much, she couldn't say no. As soon as she could, she hopped in her animal rescue vehicle and drove over to Fred's cedar log cabin.

When she arrived, she was greeted very warmly and was shown the armadillo triplets.

"I would have dug my pool somewhere else had I known the armadillos were there. But, unfortunately, I didn't," Fred said sincerely.

Fred helped Andrea load the armadillos in her car and gratefully thanked her. Fred and his wife waved to Andrea as she sped away.

Back at the Tender Heart Wildlife Rehabilitation Center, Andrea fixed up a clear glass aquarium for them to stay in. She placed brown dirt for them in the bottom and added soft sand for them to lay on. She filled a blue bowl full of fresh water. Then she put that inside their new temporary home.

She stood by the aquarium for a second wondering if she missed anything. She thought they might like a heat lamp and added that.

When placed in their new home, the armadillos, Tank, Hank, and Frank, were overjoyed by everything, especially the heat lamp! Better than that, though, was the fact that Andrea allowed them to swim in her bathtub twice a day! Armadillos love water!

After two enjoyable, fun months of playing, growing, eating, and, of course, sleeping, Andrea decided that the armadillos were big enough for a larger, outdoor home. Their new enclosed pen was spacious with plenty of room for digging up grubs, worms, and other squirmy things that armadillos consider delicacies. It was also large enough for a small kiddie pool! The armadillos had a blast while swimming laps in it!

The triplets were enjoying their new outdoor enclosure, and at the velocity they were growing, Andrea figured she could release them in the wilds of Arkansas within the following six weeks!

After two weeks, however, a massive thunderstorm struck Berryville, Arkansas, where the Tender Heart Wildlife Rehabilitation Center is located. The lightning bolts were so amazingly numerous and severe that one bolt even knocked out Andrea's electricity!

Later, when the booming thunder had turned into a quiet, dull rumble, Andrea looked out her window to see a cloudless sky. She figured it would be okay to go outside to check on the animals and do her evening chores, so she did.

As she left her house and began checking the animal's cages, she was shocked by what she saw! The armadillo's cage had been hit by a bolt of lightning! She ran over to their cage to find only one of the three alive, Tank.

Yes, he was still alive, if you could call him that. He was on his side, barely breathing!

Andrea quickly took Tank inside her rehabilitation center and laid him under a heat lamp. His heart rate was rapid and irregular.

Considering the condition he was in, Andrea didn't think he would survive the night.

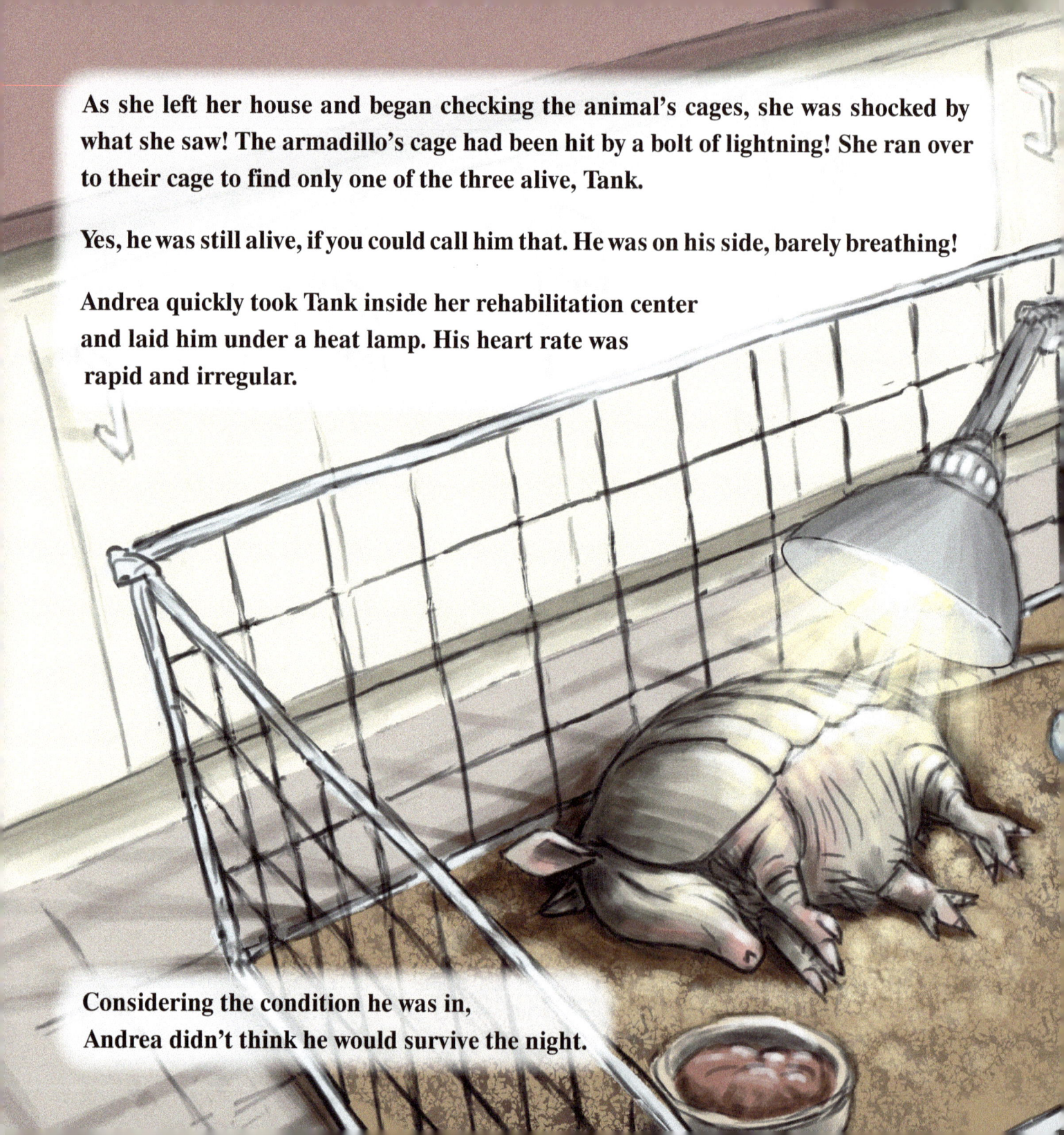

She offered a quick prayer, "Dear Jesus, please help Tank to get well. Amen."

To Andrea's amazement, by the grace of God, Tank was up on all fours in the morning looking for grubs! He had overcome the odds and showed no signs of distress.

Six weeks later, Andrea took Tank to a nearby forest to release him back to his normal habitat. With a smile on her face and a thankful heart, she watched Tank, the "tankful" armadillo, scurry back into the underbrush to begin his new life.

"My little children, let us not love in word, neither in tongue; but in deed and in truth" (1 John 3:18, KJV).

ARMADILLO FACTS:

1. Armadillos are small to medium size mammals. The smallest species, the Pink Fairy Armadillo, is roughly chipmunk-sized at 85 g (3.0 oz.) and 13–15 cm (5.1–5.9 in.) in total length. The largest species, the Giant Armadillo, can be the size of a small pig and weigh up to 54 kg (119 lb.) and be 150 cm (59 in.) long.

2. The diets of different armadillo species vary but consist mainly of insects, grubs, and other invertebrates. Some species, however, feed almost entirely on ants and termites.

3. They are prolific diggers. Many species use their sharp claws to dig for food, such as grubs, and to dig dens. The nine-banded armadillo prefers to build burrows in moist soil near the creeks, streams, and arroyos around which it lives and feeds. Armadillos do not share burrows with other adults. They usually dig a burrow 7 or 8 inches in diameter, the width of their body, and up to 15 feet in length for shelter and raising young. Armadillos live mostly in the Southeastern United States.

4. Armadillos have short legs, but they can move quickly, and they have the ability to remain underwater for as long as six minutes. An armadillo will sink in water unless it swallows air, inflating its stomach to twice its normal size and raising its buoyancy above that of water allowing it to swim. Armadillos also have poor eyesight, so they use their keen sense of smell to hunt for food. They have five clawed toes on their hind feet and three to five toes with digging claws on the forefeet. Armadillos have a low body temperature of about 33–36 degrees Celsius.

5. Young are born in nests within the burrow. The babies are born with soft, leathery skin that hardens within a few weeks. Some species only have four babies (of the same sex) but others have between one and eight. The Nine-banded Armadillos have four identical offspring as the result of a single egg.

6. **Armadillos are a source of leprosy infections in humans, particularly in Louisiana and Texas, where some people hunt, skin, and eat armadillos. Up to twenty percent of armadillos carry leprosy. In general, untrained people should not handle armadillos, and they should never be eaten.**

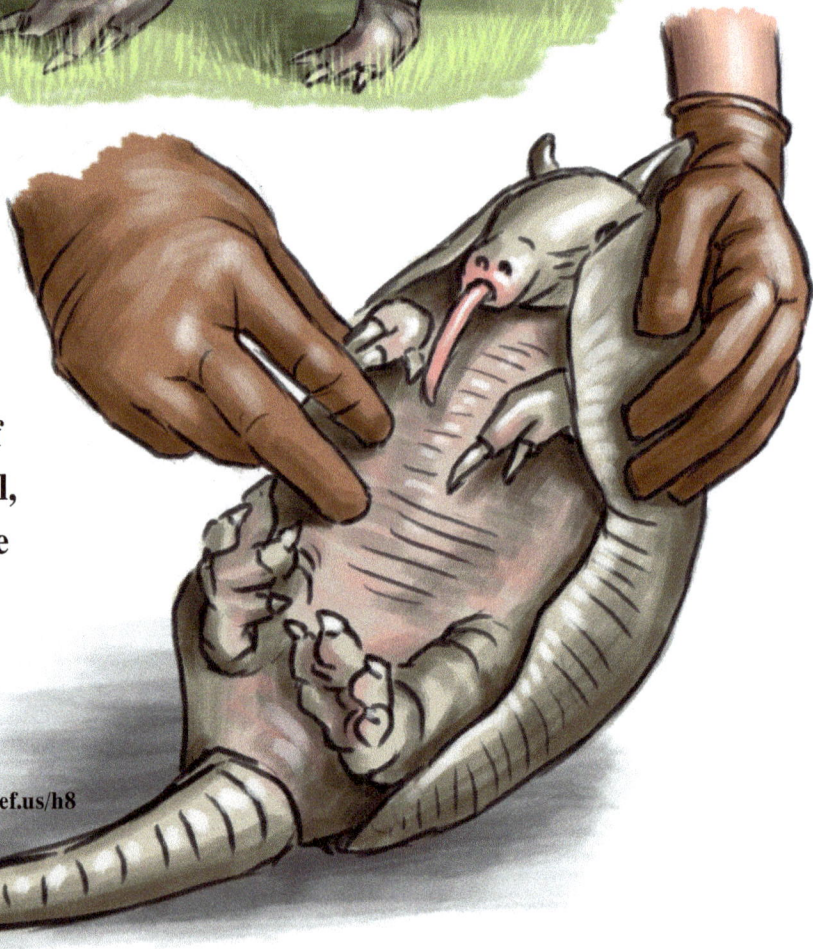

REFERENCES:
Internet Center for Wildlife Damage Management. http://1ref.us/h8
The New York Times. http://1ref.us/ha
Wikipedia. http://1ref.us/h9

7. The word armadillo means "little armored one" in Spanish. Most species have rigid shields over the shoulders and hips, with a number of bands separated by flexible skin covering the back and flanks. Additional armor covers the top of the head, the upper parts of the limbs, and the tail. The underside of the animal is never armored; it is simply covered with soft skin and fur. The armor is formed by plates of dermal bone covered in relatively small, overlapping epidermal scales called "scutes," composed of bone with a covering of horn. This armor-like skin appears to be the main defense of many armadillos, although most escape predators by fleeing (often into thorny patches, from which their armor protects them) or digging to safety. The North American nine-banded armadillo tends to jump straight in the air when surprised, and consequently, it often hits the undercarriage or fenders of passing vehicles. When threatened by a predator, the Tolypeutes species frequently roll up into a ball. Others can't roll because they have too many plates on their backs.

TIPS ON WHAT TO DO WITH AN INJURED WILD ANIMAL:

1. Never touch or pick up an injured or wild animal without asking an adult for help.

2. Never lift an injured animal unless an adult is with you and is sure you can move the animal without hurting it, yourself, or others.

3. Always wear gloves when touching a wild animal.

4. Keep the animal away from your face.

5. Wash your hands thoroughly after handling the animal.

6. Call for help if you can't reach the animal safely.

7. Never try to free an animal from a snare or trap; instead, call your local wildlife rehabilitator for assistance.

8. If you or your parents are unsure of what to do, keep a safe distance and call a vet or licensed wildlife rehabilitator, like Andrea White at Tender Heart Wildlifc Rchabilitation Center in Berryville, Arkansas, for help.